Nordstrom
Entertaining at Home Cookbook

Nordstrom
Entertaining at Home Cookbook

DELICIOUS RECIPES FOR MEMORABLE GATHERINGS

John Clem and Michael Northern

PHOTOGRAPHS BY E.J. ARMSTRONG

CHRONICLE BOOKS

SAN FRANCISCO

ISBN 0-8118-4811-6

Manufactured in China.

Design and typesetting by Gretchen Scoble
Prop styling by Patty Whittmann
Food styling by Diana Isaiou

The photographer wishes to thank The Antique Liquidator Family, Scott Pitts, and Lance Hofstad.

10 9 8 7 6 5 4 3 2 1

Published exclusively for Nordstrom, Inc., by Chronicle Books LLC.

Chronicle Books LLC
85 Second Street
San Francisco, California 94105
www.chroniclebooks.com

To the sweet memories of Maye Clem and Russell Northern.

May their spirit live on forever...

Contents

PREFACE 9

INTRODUCTION 10

Appetizers

Sherry's Pecans 15

Tomato and Goat Cheese Crepes 17

Roasted Garlic with Rosemary and Blue Cheese 18

Baked Artichoke Dip 21

Marinated Shrimp 22

My Mother's Baked Chicken Wings 24

Cheese Grits with Black Forest Ham
and Wild Mushrooms 25

Michele's Black Bean Salsa 27

Honey-Mustard Chicken Skewers 29

Vince's Salsa 30

Perfect Guacamole 31

Beverages

Mango Chill Smoothie 35

Margarita 36

Festive Sangria 38

Raspberry Revolution Smoothie 41

Lime-Mint Cooler 42

Strawberry-Watermelon Cooler 45

Salads

Asparagus and Goat Cheese Salad 49

Lime and Cilantro Chicken Salad 50

Chicken Yakisoba Salad 53

Mediterranean Chopped Salad 55

Panzanella Salad 57

Acapulco Shrimp Salad 58

Strawberry and Spinach Salad 59

Mixed Berry and Chicken Salad 60

Soups

Cream of Crab Soup 65

Chinese Hot-and-Sour Soup 66

New Orleans Seafood Gumbo 69

Summertime Gazpacho 70

Portobello Brie Soup with Fresh Sage 72

Spring Asparagus Soup 74

Grilled Corn and Shrimp Chowder 75

Main Courses

Authentic Fettuccine Alfredo 79

Cajun Cedar-Planked Salmon 80

Chilean Sea Bass with Wild Mushrooms on
Three-Cheese Polenta 83

Roasted Lamb Shanks with Currant-Apple Relish 85

Prime Rib Roast with Garlic and Rosemary 86

Chicken Paillard 88

Thai Basil Chicken   91

Fettuccine Pescatore   93

Roast Beef Tenderloin with Whipped Cream–

    Horseradish Sauce   94

Chicken Breast Poblano   95

Perfect Roasted Chicken   97

Stuffed Pork Loin with Madeira Sauce   98

From the Grill

Chili-Marinated Flank Steak   103

Asian-Style Grilled Vegetables   104

Cilantro-Lime Grilled Chicken   106

Rosemary and Thyme Grilled Lamb Chops   109

Teriyaki Grilled Salmon with Asian Salsa   111

Grilled Chicken with Orange-Ginger Glaze   112

Grilled Halibut and Chestnut Street Grill Tartar Sauce   113

Grilled Shrimp with Dark Cherry–Ginger Glaze   114

Bone-In Rib Eye with Blue Cheese Butter   117

Potluck

Sunday Fried Chicken   121

Sylvia's Apple Bread   123

Ev's Olives   124

Brunch Banana Bread   126

Field Family Coleslaw   127

Vine-Ripe Vegetable Salad with Feta Cheese   129

Tabbouleh Salad   130

Spicy Chicken Chili   131

Focaccia with Kalamata Olives   132

Sausage and Peppers with Orzo   135

Side Dishes

Jeannie's Carrots   139

Sautéed Snap Peas and Shiitake Mushrooms

    with Soy Sauce   140

Healthy Sautéed Spinach   142

Chinois Rice   143

Green Beans Provençal   144

Parmesan–Scalloped Potato Gratin   146

Crispy Roasted Potatoes and Wilted Greens   149

Desserts

Madeline Cake   153

Summer Berry Shortcake   155

Southern Pecan Pie   156

Key Lime Pie   159

Lily Rose's White Chocolate Banana Cream Pie   160

Sinful Chocolate Torte   162

Bistro Profiteroles   164

Country Apple-Coconut Cake   166

Pearl's Chocolate Chip and Walnut Pound Cake   167

Chocolate Mousse   168

Dried Cherry–Oatmeal Cookies   171

Chocolate Velvet Pie   172

INDEX   173

ACKNOWLEDGMENTS   176

Preface

Some of my happiest memories revolve around get-togethers with family and friends. At the heart of these recollections are the fabulous meals built from wonderful ingredients and set in a heartwarming atmosphere.

This book follows on the heels of our first cookbook, *Nordstrom Friends and Family,* which many of our cherished customers now have. Here, as before, the recipes come from Nordstrom employees from around the country who are generously sharing their favorite dishes for all of us to enjoy. Each recipe includes a brief story of how it is particularly well suited to entertaining friends and family, a principle that fits perfectly with our commitment to treating our customers with humble warmth and great service.

Food and beverage service is an important element of the customer experience in our stores. Our restaurant and specialty coffee professionals have become a leading force in the food-service industry by delivering uniquely wonderful experiences in our cafes and coffee bars. This book serves as an important point of connection between our apparel and shoe business and the world of food-service hospitality.

Here's a toast from our family to yours: May your get-togethers be filled with delicious food and boundless happiness.

—BRUCE NORDSTROM
Chairman

Introduction

Entertaining through the sharing of food is firmly rooted in the act of honoring and nurturing those we care about and admire. This simple belief is the driving force behind this collection of recipes for our customers to use at home. We did not set out to compose a how-to guide to planning, preparing, and staging parties. Instead, we gathered recipes from Nordstrom employees, each one with its own story. Many of these tales relate how a dish marked an important moment or celebration in the contributor's life, and every one of them is rich in heartwarming tradition.

The most memorable part of any gathering is the delivery of surprising flavors in simply prepared dishes. This book offers a collection of recipes that helps the reader find an easy path to entertaining, while having fun and gaining inspiration at the same time. Instead of presenting a checklist from menu to décor, we are humbly sharing a carefully selected collection of timeless recipes that are guaranteed to wow the guests at your next party. We believe that the simpler the dish, the greater the potential for its success, so throughout this book you will find freshly prepared dishes made from high-quality everyday ingredients.

Entertaining is as much about spending quality time with your guests as it is about serving satisfying beverages and flavorful foods. By combining ease of preparation with delicious results, we are enabling you to carve out more time with your guests, which ultimately makes any gathering more successful. If too much effort is made to coordinate, prepare, and present dishes, your guests may feel uncomfortable. Simply put, get-togethers are most successful when the host or hostess mingles among the company, sharing in the precious moments of conversation and interaction.

Our stores have been a wonderful environment for growing and nurturing a culture of food-service hospitality over the more than two dozen years of Nordstrom Restaurants. Learning how to build and expand different food-service concepts within our retail stores has provided us with unforgettable lifetime memories. Our cafes and coffee bars are warm and vital gathering places within our stores. Nordstrom's passion for customer service provides us with a natural "frame" for our picture of restaurant hospitality. This same passion drives us to support the many talented people who work in our food and coffee operations—all of them dedicated to high standards of food, coffee, and customer service.

Embarking on the creation of a second cookbook was a natural path for all of us at Nordstrom. Our first endeavor, *Nordstrom Friends and Family Cookbook,* taught us how relevant it was to broadcast a message of culinary excellence. *Nordstrom Entertaining at Home Cookbook* carries that same message but is also designed to help our customers give their guests the ultimate gift of sharing wonderful food at home. Few things are more memorable than the surprising tastes of simply prepared dishes that beg the question "How did you do that?"

Food is the universal welcome, so entertaining with food will always be an important element in our lives. Some of our most cherished childhood memories hang on the sweet image of sneaking into the main room before or during a gathering, under the radar screen of our parents, and sampling the many colorful dishes on the table. We fondly remember our parents successfully balancing the serving of great food with warm and lively conversation. Such memories become more precious to us over time.

It is our hope that when you try these recipes they will provide you with both inspiration and success. Tradition is born of wonderful memories that start with a single experience. We pass these recipes, along with their stories, to you with the hope that you will share them with your family and friends.

—John Clem and Michael Northern

APPETIZERS

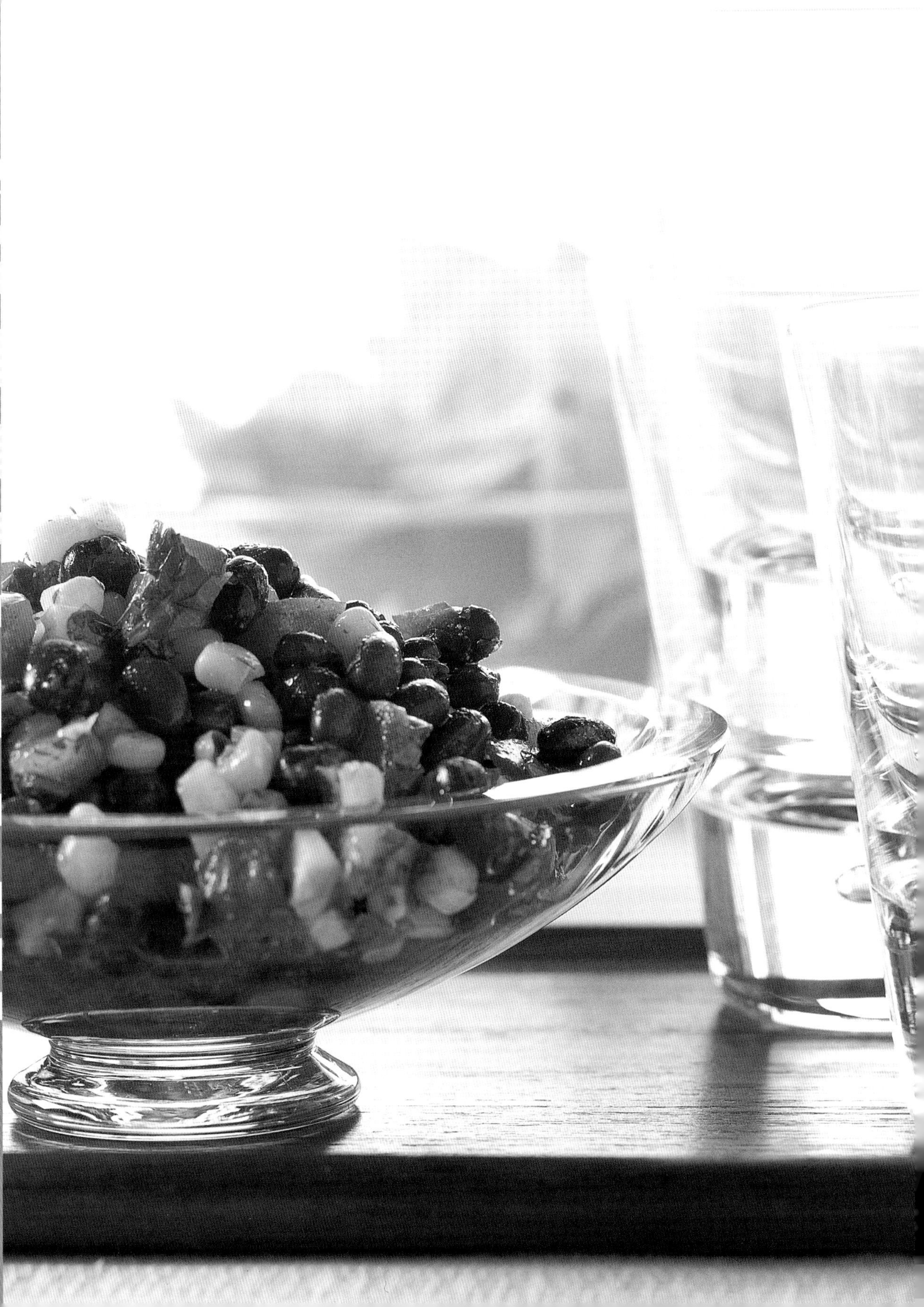

Appetizers can open the hearth of your home to guests better than any other course in the meal. Often, they can provide the spark that encourages people to talk and interact, breaking the ice of unfamiliarity. They can wake up your guests' appetites, too. Or, they can simply provide a savory companion to that glass of wine or other beverage that begins a celebration.

The recipes that follow are a good mix of seafood, chicken, and vegetarian fare, and focus on both ease of preparation and showstopping presentation. Experiment using elements of your menu to decorate the table, such as a bowl heaped with artichokes or limes when featuring a dish that calls for that ingredient. Sometimes something as simple as a bowl of assorted whole fruits floating in ice water can be attractive and memorable.

Sherry's Pecans

↔ makes about 6 cups

I first discovered this recipe nearly thirty years ago when my son was in a Montessori preschool. A group of us mothers would get together at Sherry's house for yoga and desserts while our kids were at school. Since that time, I have made these pecans often, and they have become a frequently requested snack from my friends and family. They are also popular holiday gifts. This recipe delivers all the flavors of a sticky pecan roll without any of the mess! GERRY WELLER

Unsalted butter for preparing baking sheet

1 large egg white

1 tablespoon water

1 cup sugar

1 teaspoon ground cinnamon

1 teaspoon kosher salt

1 pound pecan halves

Preheat the oven to 225°F. Lightly butter a rimmed baking sheet.

In a small bowl, whisk the egg white with the water until the mixture is completely foamy and no liquid remains.

In a separate bowl, stir together the sugar, cinnamon, and salt.

Add the pecans to the egg white mixture and toss gently to coat. Sprinkle the sugar-cinnamon mixture over the pecan mixture and stir to combine evenly. Scatter the pecans on the prepared baking sheet, arranging them in a single layer.

Bake the pecans, stirring them with a spatula every 15 minutes or so, until they are a rich brown and nicely glazed, about 1 hour. Remove from the oven and, using a metal spatula, transfer the pecans to a large platter, arranging them in a single layer.

Serve the pecans warm, or let cool completely and store in a covered container at room temperature for up to 3 days.

Tomato and Goat Cheese Crepes

↔ serves 8

Even though this elegant appetizer requires some work to put together, I find that I can get quite a bit of it done ahead of time, so that all that's left to do when my guests arrive is pop the crepes in the oven to heat through. I guess because I started my culinary career as a pastry chef, I find comfort in working with recipes that can be assembled in advance. CHEF BETSY BELL

CREPE BATTER

1$^1/_2$ cups milk

2 large eggs

$^3/_4$ cup plus 2 tablespoons all-purpose flour

2 teaspoons unsalted butter, melted, plus more
    melted butter for cooking crepes

$^3/_4$ teaspoon kosher salt

$^3/_4$ teaspoon freshly ground black pepper

FILLING

$^1/_4$ pound fresh goat cheese, at room temperature,
    lightly whipped with a fork

3 plum tomatoes, cored and cut into sixteen
    $^1/_4$ -inch-thick slices

Kosher salt

Freshly ground black pepper

Unsalted butter, melted, for brushing
    baking sheets and crepes

$^1/_2$ cup chopped green onion, white and light green
    part only

2 tablespoons balsamic vinegar

2 tablespoons extra-virgin olive oil

Preheat the oven to 350ºF. To make the Crepe Batter, in a blender, combine the milk, eggs, flour, 2 teaspoons melted butter, salt, and pepper. Process on medium speed until well combined and no lumps remain, 15 to 20 seconds.

Place a 9-inch nonstick skillet over low to medium-low heat. When the pan is hot, brush it lightly with melted butter and lift from the stove. Pour $^1/_4$ cup of the batter into the center of the pan, and then working quickly, tilt and rotate the pan to cover the bottom evenly with the batter. Return the pan to medium-low heat and cook until the batter sets and the bottom of the crepe is lightly browned, about 1 minute. Using a spatula, flip the crepe over and continue cooking until cooked through, 30 to 45 seconds longer. Transfer the finished crepe to a plate. Adjust the temperature of the heat if necessary and repeat with the remaining batter to produce 8 crepes in all, brushing the pan with more butter as needed to prevent burning. As the crepes are cooked, stack them. Let cool for about 10 minutes before filling them.

To fill the crepes, lay 1 crepe, with the more attractive side facing down, on a clean work surface. Using a flexible spatula, evenly spread about 1$^1/_2$ tablespoons of the goat cheese on the lower half of the crepe, taking care not to tear the crepe. Place 2 tomato slices side by side on top of the goat cheese, and season the tomato slices with salt and pepper. Fold the upper half of the crepe over onto the goat cheese and tomato slices, covering completely. Fold the halved crepe in half again, creating a quarter circle. Set aside and repeat to create 8 filled and folded crepes in all.

Lightly brush a rimmed baking sheet with melted butter, and arrange the folded crepes, evenly spaced, on the pan. Brush the tops lightly with melted butter and bake until the filling is heated through and the crepes are delicately browned, 10 to 12 minutes.

Remove the crepes from the oven and, using a metal spatula, transfer them to warmed small plates. Sprinkle each crepe with 1 tablespoon of the green onion and then drizzle each crepe with about $^3/_4$ teaspoon each vinegar and olive oil. Serve immediately.

Roasted Garlic with Rosemary and Blue Cheese ↔ serves 10 to 12

I don't remember the origin of this recipe, but I do remember the first time I made it. My husband and I went away to the ocean for a long weekend, where we found an old caboose that had been converted into a one-room getaway. Not only was it right on the ocean, but it also included a wood-burning stove and a tiny kitchen. It was like being a kid again. The evening was stormy and the place seemed magical. For supper, I threw this dish together along with a simple salad, some great bread, and a chilled bottle of Chardonnay. Since that time I have shared this dish with family and friends on many occasions, always to rave reviews. BONNIE BENDER

6 large heads garlic

2 tablespoons extra-virgin olive oil

Kosher salt

Freshly ground black pepper

2 tablespoons unsalted butter

3 rosemary sprigs, each 6 inches long

$^{1}/_{2}$ cup Chardonnay

$^{1}/_{2}$ cup vegetable broth

$^{1}/_{4}$ pound blue cheese, crumbled

Warmed baguette slices for serving

Preheat the oven to 350°F. Trim away any stray roots from the garlic heads, then carefully cut a slice off of the opposite end to expose the cloves. Rub the trimmed garlic heads with the olive oil and season them with a sprinkle of salt and pepper.

Place the prepared garlic heads, cut side up, in a small baking dish. Set 1 teaspoon butter on top of each head. Remove the leaves from 1 rosemary sprig and chop finely. Sprinkle the rosemary evenly over the garlic heads. Place the 2 remaining sprigs between the heads. Pour the Chardonnay and the broth into the dish, and scatter the blue cheese all around the heads.

Bake the garlic heads, basting the tops with pan juices every 20 minutes, for 1$^{1}/_{2}$ hours. The garlic is done when it is lightly browned and you can easily pierce it with a paring knife, and the broth and wine are reduced.

Let cool slightly and serve directly from the dish, accompanied with the bread. To eat, diners pull apart the garlic heads into individual cloves, squeeze the softened garlic onto the baguette slices, spread it evenly, and then spoon some of the cheese mixture on top.

Baked Artichoke Dip

↔ serves 12 to 14

I developed this recipe specifically for this cookbook, as I wanted to ensure that we offered a casual dip that delivers a big, full flavor. I started with the thought that artichokes go well with roasted peppers and that roasted peppers go well with basil and that basil goes well with Parmesan—well, you get the idea. One thing led to another and out of the oven popped this delicious and memorable dip. Serve it alongside Vince's Salsa (page 30) and offer them both with crisp corn tortilla chips.

CHEF CHRISTOPHER SMITH

1 cup mayonnaise

3/4 cup sour cream

2 cups (8 ounces) freshly grated Parmesan cheese,
      preferably Parmigiano-Reggiano

3 tablespoons cider vinegar

2 tablespoons chopped fresh basil

2 cloves garlic, minced

1 teaspoon kosher salt

1 teaspoon freshly ground black pepper

2 cans (13 1/2 ounces each) artichoke hearts,
      drained and coarsely chopped

1 red bell pepper, roasted, peeled, seeded, and
      chopped (see Cook's Note)

1 can (7 ounces) diced green chiles, drained

Preheat the oven to 350°F.

In a bowl, combine the mayonnaise, sour cream, 1 1/2 cups of the Parmesan cheese, the vinegar, basil, garlic, salt, and pepper. Stir until well combined. Using a rubber spatula, gently fold in the artichokes, bell pepper, and chiles. Transfer to a decorative baking dish and, using the spatula, smooth the surface. Scatter the remaining 1/2 cup Parmesan cheese evenly over the top.

Bake, uncovered, until lightly browned and gently bubbling around the edges, about 45 minutes. Remove from the oven and let cool for 5 minutes before serving directly from the dish.

COOK'S NOTE: *To roast and peel bell peppers or chiles, prepare a medium-hot fire in a charcoal grill, or preheat a gas grill on medium-high. Place the bell peppers or chiles directly over the fire and roast, turning when each side has blistered and blackened, for 2 to 3 minutes per side, or 10 to 12 minutes total. Alternatively, prepare the bell peppers or chiles the same way by placing them directly over a gas burner on your stove top. Transfer the roasted peppers or chiles to a small bowl, cover tightly with plastic wrap, and let them rest until they are cool enough to handle, about 15 minutes. Peel away the skins, then slit lengthwise and remove the stems, seeds, and ribs. Cut as directed in individual recipes.*

Marinated Shrimp

↔ serves 8 to 10

This recipe has been a family favorite for many years for a trio of reasons: it bursts with flavor, is easy to prepare ahead, and is just dressy enough to impress an audience. We serve it at most of our big gatherings, such as birthdays, holidays, and house-warming parties. Days later, it is not uncommon for some of the partygoers to ask, "Who made that delicious shrimp?" Now you can say that you did! LISA BARELA

COOKED SHRIMP

2 quarts water

2 bay leaves

2 tablespoons Old Bay seasoning

$1/2$ teaspoon whole black peppercorns

1 tablespoon kosher salt

1 clove garlic, smashed

1 lemon, halved

2 pounds large shrimp, split and deveined
     with shell intact

MARINADE

$1/2$ cup extra-virgin olive oil

$1/4$ cup dry white wine

$1/4$ cup fresh lemon juice

$1^1/2$ teaspoons minced garlic

$1/4$ cup Dijon mustard

$1/4$ cup chopped fresh flat-leaf parsley

$1/4$ cup minced shallots

$1^1/2$ teaspoons kosher salt

$1/2$ teaspoon red pepper flakes

Freshly ground black pepper

To prepare the Cooked Shrimp, in a 4-quart saucepan, combine the water, bay leaves, Old Bay seasoning, peppercorns, salt, and garlic. Squeeze the juice from the lemon halves into the pan and then add the spent halves. Place the pan over medium-high heat and bring to a boil. Add the shrimp, reduce the heat to low, and cook uncovered, stirring once, until the shrimp turn uniformly pink and all of the translucence is gone from the thickest part of the bodies, about 4 minutes, depending on the size of the shrimp. Drain the shrimp into a colander. Let cool completely, and then peel off the shells, leaving the tail segments intact. Cover and refrigerate until needed.

To make the Marinade, in a bowl, combine the olive oil, wine, lemon juice, garlic, mustard, parsley, shallots, salt, red pepper flakes, and a few grinds of black pepper. Whisk the ingredients together until well combined, then taste and adjust seasoning.

Place the cooked shrimp in a 1-gallon lock-top plastic bag or in a shallow dish. Pour the marinade over the shrimp, coating them well. Squeeze all of the air out of the bag and seal it, or cover the dish. Refrigerate for at least 4 hours or for up to 24 hours.

Transfer the shrimp (and marinade) to a serving bowl and serve well chilled.

My Mother's Baked Chicken Wings

↔ serves 12 to 14

Even though the recipe is simple, my mother always receives rave reviews for her chicken wings. Look for good-sized drumettes, as they stand up to the long baking time better. No matter how hard I try, or how accurate my recipe, somehow these always taste better when my mom cooks them. The wings can be served either hot or cold, though I doubt that there will be any left to get cold! CHEF CHRISTOPHER SMITH

3^1/$_2$ pounds chicken wing drumettes

1 cup soy sauce

^{1}/$_3$ cup dry vermouth

^{1}/$_4$ cup peanut oil

3 tablespoons sugar

3 cloves garlic, minced

1 tablespoon peeled, minced fresh ginger

Place the chicken wings in a 1-gallon lock-top plastic bag or in a shallow dish. In a small bowl, combine the soy sauce, vermouth, peanut oil, sugar, garlic, and ginger and whisk until well blended. Pour the marinade over the chicken wings, coating them well. Squeeze all of the air out of the bag and seal it, or cover the dish. Refrigerate and marinate for at least 12 hours or for up to 24 hours, turning the bag or stirring the chicken wings once to distribute the flavors evenly.

Preheat the oven to 300°F. Transfer the wings and all the marinade to a rimmed baking sheet, spreading out the wings in an even layer. Bake the wings, turning them over every 20 minutes or so to ensure even glazing, until they are a rich brown color and cooked through, about 1^1/$_2$ hours.

Remove the pan from the oven and let the wings rest for 2 minutes, and then, using a spatula, transfer to a serving platter. Serve immediately.

Cheese Grits with Black Forest Ham and Wild Mushrooms ↔ serves 8 to 10

This recipe combines the silky texture of grits with the bold flavor of Black Forest ham and the earthy flavors of roasted mush-rooms. The secret to its success is to be forceful when seasoning the mushrooms. They need to be exceptionally flavorful in order to harmonize with the Black Forest ham and stand out against the grits. Although you can substitute a more basic ham for the Black Forest, I feel that it's worth seeking out the genuine article for this dish. Purchase the ham in thicker slices, about ⅛ inch, and cut into thin julienne strips of the same width for taste and appearance. MICHAEL NORTHERN

ROASTED MUSHROOMS

1 pound shiitake mushrooms, stems discarded
  and large caps halved

1 pound cremini mushrooms, stems trimmed
  and large caps halved

¼ cup extra-virgin olive oil

2 teaspoons seasoned salt

1 teaspoon granulated garlic

1 teaspoon granulated onion

½ teaspoon freshly ground black pepper

CHEDDAR CHEESE GRITS

1 can (49 ounces) low-sodium beef broth

Kosher salt

1½ cups medium-grind grits

3 tablespoons unsalted butter

1 cup (about 4 ounces) finely shredded sharp white
  Cheddar cheese

Freshly ground black pepper

½ pound Black Forest ham, julienned

Position a rack in the upper third of the oven and preheat to 450°F.

To make the Roasted Mushrooms, in a large bowl, combine the shiitake and cremini mushrooms. Drizzle with the olive oil and toss to coat evenly. In a small bowl, stir together the seasoned salt, garlic, onion, and pepper. Sprinkle the seasoning mixture over the mushroom mixture and toss to coat evenly.

Transfer the mushrooms to a large rimmed baking sheet, spreading them out in a thin, even layer. Roast in the oven, undisturbed, until nicely browned and tender, 14 to 16 minutes. Remove from the oven and set aside in a warm place. Do not cover the mushrooms, or they will leach moisture.

While the mushrooms are roasting, make the Cheddar Cheese Grits: Pour the broth into a heavy 4-quart saucepan and bring to a boil over medium-high heat. Reduce the heat to medium-low and add 1 teaspoon salt. Whisking constantly, add the grits in a slow, steady stream. Adjust the heat so that the grits do not splatter, and cook, stirring frequently, until all of the water is absorbed and the mixture is creamy, 16 to 18 minutes.

Remove the grits from the heat and stir in the butter and cheese. Season to taste with salt and pepper. Gently fold in the ham.

Spoon the grit mixture into warmed pasta bowls or a large serving dish and scatter the warm roasted mushrooms over the top. Serve at once.

Michele's Black Bean Salsa

↔ serves 10 to 12

My family has moved frequently, so extending our hand in friendship has been my focus when adjusting to a new city. Our current residence in Seattle, Washington, has turned out to be a social phenomenon, resulting in our socializing with four other families in our cul-de-sac at least twice a week. Each family brings a couple of dishes to share and I usually bring my now-famous black bean salsa. It's a hit every time! MICHELE LOVE

2 ears corn, shucked and grilled or boiled

2 cans (14 ounces each) black beans, rinsed
      and drained

$1/3$ cup fresh lime juice

$1/3$ cup canola oil

$1/4$ cup minced red onion

$1/4$ cup minced green onion, white and
      light green part only

$1 1/2$ teaspoons ground cumin

$1 1/2$ tablespoons Cajun seasoning

1 cup chopped tomatoes

$1/2$ cup chopped fresh cilantro

Kosher salt

Freshly ground black pepper

2 avocados, halved, pitted, peeled, and diced

Working with 1 ear of corn at a time, stand it upright, stem end down, on a cutting board. Using a sharp knife, cut downward along the cob, removing the kernels and rotating the cob a quarter turn after each cut. Discard the cobs and scoop the kernels into a large bowl. You should have about $1 1/2$ cups.

Add the black beans, lime juice, canola oil, red onion, green onion, cumin, Cajun seasoning, tomatoes, and cilantro and stir to combine. Season to taste with salt and pepper. Gently fold in the avocado. Serve immediately, or cover with plastic wrap and refrigerate for up to 4 hours before serving.

Honey-Mustard Chicken Skewers

↔ makes 6 to 8 skewers

Every time I grill these chicken skewers at a barbecue, they are the first things to disappear from the table. It's funny how the simplest dishes often make the biggest impression at any event! The marinade not only makes these skewers look great, but it also guarantees that the chicken always turns out sweet, moist, and delicious. The marinade can do double duty as a dipping sauce, or do as I do and reserve some to drizzle over the skewers when they are hot off the grill. TINA DEVLIN

1 cup mayonnaise

1 tablespoon Dijon mustard

1 tablespoon honey

$1/2$ teaspoon garlic powder

$1/2$ teaspoon kosher salt

$1/2$ teaspoon freshly ground black pepper

1 clove garlic, finely minced

$1^1/2$ pounds boneless, skinless chicken breasts, cut into 1-inch pieces

Vegetable oil for brushing

In a bowl, combine the mayonnaise, mustard, honey, garlic powder, salt, pepper, and garlic. Whisk to combine. Measure out $1/4$ cup of the mixture, cover, and refrigerate until needed.

Place the chicken pieces in a 1-gallon lock-top plastic bag or in a shallow dish. Pour the remaining honey-mustard mixture over them, coating well. Squeeze all of the air out of the bag and seal it, or cover the dish. Refrigerate for at least 4 hours or for up to 24 hours, turning the bag or stirring the chicken once to distribute the marinade evenly.

About 2 hours before you are ready to begin grilling, put 6 to 8 bamboo skewers, each 8 inches long, in water to soak.

Prepare a medium-hot fire in a charcoal grill, or preheat a gas grill on medium-high. Drain the skewers. Remove the chicken pieces from the marinade and thread them on the skewers, dividing the pieces evenly. Brush the grill grate with vegetable oil.

Place the skewers directly over the fire. Cover the grill and cook on one side for about 6 minutes, checking occasionally to make sure the chicken isn't burning. Turn the skewers over, re-cover the grill, and continue cooking until the chicken is tender and opaque throughout, about 5 minutes longer.

Arrange the skewers on a serving platter and drizzle the reserved honey-mustard mixture over the top. Serve immediately.

Vince's Salsa

↔ serves 12 to 14

One of my favorite pastimes is eating fiery chiles of any sort—the hotter the better. For years now, I have been growing a wide range of chiles at home with great success. My only problem is what to do with them all when they are harvested. This recipe, however, is about salsa that is decidedly mild. Its success relies on the balance of ingredients and great texture, rather than chile heat. I like to allow it to rest for 2 to 4 hours before serving so the flavors have time to develop. Not only does the salsa improve, but I get the chance to do other things before my guests arrive. Of course, you can make the salsa a little wilder by adding more jalapeño chile. Serve with a fresh batch of tortilla chips. VINCENT ROSSETTI

6 plum tomatoes, cored, diced, and well drained
    in a sieve (about 3 cups)

2 cans (14$^1/_2$ ounces each) diced tomatoes in juice,
    well drained in a sieve

$^1/_2$ cup tomato purée

$^3/_4$ cup minced red onion

$^1/_2$ cup chopped green onion, white and light green
    part only

$^1/_2$ cup chopped yellow bell pepper

$^1/_2$ cup chopped red bell pepper

1 jalapeño chile, seeded, deribbed, and finely
    minced

2 cloves garlic, minced

1 tablespoon fresh lemon juice

1 tablespoon fresh lime juice

1 tablespoon Tabasco sauce

1 teaspoon ground cumin, lightly toasted
    (see Cook's Note)

1 teaspoon kosher salt

$^1/_2$ teaspoon freshly ground black pepper

$^1/_4$ cup chopped fresh cilantro

In a bowl, combine the fresh plum tomatoes, canned diced tomatoes, tomato purée, red onion, green onion, yellow and red bell pepper, jalapeño chile, garlic, lemon juice, lime juice, Tabasco, cumin, salt, and pepper. Stir to mix well, then taste and adjust the seasoning. Add the cilantro and stir until evenly distributed.

Transfer to a decorative serving bowl, cover with plastic wrap, and refrigerate for at least 2 hours or for up to 4 hours to allow the flavors to develop before serving. Serve chilled or at room temperature.

COOK'S NOTE: *Toasting the cumin releases some of its stored flavors and refreshes its fragrance. Simply measure what you need into a nonstick skillet and warm it over very low heat until you notice the aroma, about 45 seconds.*

Perfect Guacamole

↔ serves 6 to 8

I have never really followed a recipe for guacamole. It just seems to flow naturally as I prepare it—a pinch of this, a scoop of that. The recipe here is an attempt to quantify those instincts. You must also start with perfectly ripe avocados of good quality. If an avocado is too ripe, your guacamole will have no texture, while if it is too firm, it will have no flavor. I always use Hass avocados for their buttery texture and nutty flavor, and I admit to checking nearly every one at the produce market in order to find the perfect specimens for my guacamole. This flavorful, traditional recipe, with its festive colors and hint of fresh cilantro, works beautifully. VINCENT ROSSETTI

6 large, ripe Hass avocados, halved, pitted, peeled, and diced

1 firm and ripe tomato, cored and chopped (about 1 cup)

$1/3$ cup minced red onion

1 clove garlic, finely minced

$1/2$ jalapeño chile, seeded, deribbed, and finely minced

2 tablespoons fresh lime juice

2 tablespoons chopped fresh cilantro

$1/4$ cup sour cream

$1/2$ teaspoon Tabasco sauce

$1/2$ teaspoon kosher salt

$1/4$ teaspoon freshly ground black pepper

Place half of the diced avocado in a bowl and, using the bottom of a kitchen spoon, lightly mash it, breaking up the large chunks. Add the tomato, onion, garlic, jalapeño chile, lime juice, cilantro, sour cream, Tabasco, salt, pepper, and the remaining diced avocado and stir gently to combine. Taste and adjust the seasoning.

Transfer the mixture to an attractive serving bowl. Serve immediately, or cover with plastic wrap, pressing the wrap tight against the surface of the dip to force out all the air (this will help prevent it from turning brown), and store, refrigerated, for up to 4 hours before serving.

BEVERAGES

Entertaining at home begins the moment your guests walk through the front door. And there is no better way to get things off to a rousing start than to offer them a festive beverage that is easy to make and serve. A special drink that your guests have never tried before helps break the ice among strangers. They tend to engage with one another with greater warmth and connectivity, making the event more fun from the start.

These simple recipes will arm you with a good range of choices of both alcoholic and nonalcoholic drinks. You will find everything from refreshing fruit smoothies for hot summer afternoons to a traditional sangria guaranteed to spice up any celebration. All of the recipes deliver big flavors, yet are simple and quick to make, allowing you to enjoy the festivities along with your guests. Cheers!

Mango Chili Smoothie

When we first decided to introduce smoothies at Nordstrom, we traveled across America to find the perfect smoothie, the perfect technique, and all the possible ingredients. We found our perfect smoothie in Boston and learned that it was critical to start with a great sorbet (we always use Häagen-Dazs) and to use frozen fruit to provide a good flavor and texture base. The final secret ingredient is the addition of a little ice to provide a counterpoint to the density of the fruit. Build the drink (pictured on page 32) in your blender in the sequence presented. The order makes a difference in the final results. And don't let the fruit or sorbet thaw out. You want their frozen texture. JOHN CLEM

1¼ cups fresh orange juice

1 tablespoon fresh lime juice

2 cups individually quick-frozen mango chunks

1 cup Häagen-Dazs mango sorbet

⅓ cup crushed ice

In a blender with a powerful motor, first place the orange juice, followed by the lime juice, and then the frozen mango chunks. Next add the mango sorbet and top with the ice. Cover the blender securely and process on high speed until a tornado-like vortex forms in the center of the mixture, 35 seconds or longer. Let the vortex swirl for 10 to 15 seconds longer to allow the drink to smooth out.

Pour into tall glasses and accompany with sturdy straws. Serve immediately.

Margarita

↔ serves 4 to 6

Making margaritas always creates a festive feeling as guests gather around to watch them go together. This delicious version uses plenty of fresh lime and only the classic ingredients. Served over ice cubes, the margarita is a time-honored treat. Be ready to blend many batches of this traditional version of Mexico's favorite cocktail. Your audience is bound to appreciate the smooth balance this recipe delivers. JOHN CLEM

1 cup gold tequila

1 cup Cointreau

1 cup fresh lime juice, plus 1 or 2 lime wedges
    or additional juice in a shallow bowl

$1/4$ cup superfine sugar

Kosher salt for dipping glass rims

6 cups ice cubes

In a blender, combine the tequila, Cointreau, 1 cup lime juice, and sugar. Cover and process on high speed until the sugar dissolves and the mixture is thoroughly combined, about 10 seconds.

Spread a layer of salt on a small, flat plate. Rub the rim of a glass with a lime wedge, or dip the rim in lime juice. Then dip the rim into the salt to coat lightly. Repeat with the remaining glasses. Fill each glass three-fourths full with the ice. Pour in the blended mixture, filling almost to the rim. Serve at once.

Festive Sangria

A frosty pitcher of sangria is always a festive centerpiece. Its lush flavors deepen with time, so prepare it in advance to let the fruits infuse this classic Spanish drink. Few beverages will complement your gathering as colorfully as this one. It can be served with a variety of menus, indoors or outdoors, but it is especially wonderful on warm summer nights. JOHN CLEM

1 bottle (750 ml) red wine

1 bottle (750 ml) white wine

1/2 cup light rum

1 cup fresh orange juice

1 cup fresh lime juice

1 cup superfine sugar

1 orange, sliced crosswise

1 lime, sliced crosswise

1 lemon, sliced crosswise

1 apple, cored and sliced crosswise

Ice cubes

In a large bowl, combine the wines, rum, orange juice, and lime juice. Add the sugar and stir with a large spoon until the sugar dissolves. Add the orange, lime, lemon, and apple slices and cover the bowl with plastic wrap. Refrigerate overnight or for up to 12 hours.

Using a ladle, transfer the sangria to attractive serving pitchers, distributing the fruit evenly. Add ice to each pitcher and serve well chilled in attractive tumblers or any decorative glasses.

Raspberry Revolution Smoothie

↔ makes two 1½-cup servings or three 1-cup servings

While the popularity of smoothies has made it easy to find individually quick-frozen fruits and berries in most supermarkets, sometimes they aren't readily available. Here's an easy remedy: Cover a rimmed baking sheet with plastic wrap. Arrange the desired measure of sliced fruit or berries on the prepared sheet in a single layer, and slip the sheet into the freezer to freeze the slices, 2 to 4 hours. You can use this easy technique for other common fruits that you are unable to purchase individually quick-frozen, or you can extend it to fruits that you rarely find frozen, such as locally grown peaches or nectarines. Serve this thick, flavorful smoothie for a brunch or enjoy out on the deck on a sweltering August day. JOHN CLEM

1¼ cups apple juice

1 cup individually quick-frozen strawberries

1 cup individually quick-frozen raspberries

1 cup Häagen-Dazs raspberry sorbet
    (see Headnote, page 35)

⅓ cup crushed ice cubes

In a blender with a powerful motor, first place the apple juice, followed by the frozen strawberries, and then the frozen raspberries. Next add the raspberry sorbet and top with the ice. Cover the blender securely and blend on high speed until a tornado-like vortex forms in the center of the mixture, 35 seconds or longer. Let the vortex swirl for 10 to 15 seconds longer to allow the drink to smooth out.

Pour into tall glasses and accompany with sturdy straws. Serve immediately.

Lime Mint Cooler

↪ serves 8 to 10

Served tall and cool over ice cubes, this delightfully refreshing cocktail is a favorite for any special summer occasion. You can mix it up in advance and refrigerate it so you won't have to be chained to the blender all evening. This drink tastes more like a complex cocktail from a tropical place than a three-minute blend-and-pour cooler. Everyone will rave about it! JOHN CLEM

1 can (12 ounces) frozen limeade concentrate

4^{1}/$_{2}$ cups water

^{1}/$_{2}$ cup fresh mint leaves, plus 8 to 10 sprigs
    for garnish

1^{1}/$_{4}$ cups vodka

Ice cubes

8 to 10 lime slices

In a blender with a powerful motor, combine the frozen limeade and water. Cover the blender securely and process on high speed until well combined, about 15 seconds. Add the mint leaves and pulse until the mint is just chopped, about 5 seconds. Pour the mixture into a pitcher, add the vodka, and stir well.

Fill tall glasses with ice and pour in the limeade mixture. Garnish each serving with a mint sprig and a lime slice. Serve immediately.

Strawberry-Watermelon Cooler

↔ serves 8 to 10

When you work in the kitchen all day as I do, you need an easy way to kick off a party once you get home. This drink has become our signature summer beverage because it is cool and refreshing, and it is a snap to put together. Your friends will think you spent all day on it when they see the tall frosted glasses topped with a fun, colorful garnish of watermelon wedges and mint.

CHEF MATT LICHLYTER

$^1/_2$ seedless watermelon (about 3 pounds), rind removed and cut into chunks (about 8 cups), plus 8 to 10 small wedges with rind for garnish

2 pints strawberries, hulled (about 4$^1/_2$ cups)

1$^1/_4$ cups fresh lemon juice

1 cup sugar

8 cups water

Ice cubes

1 bunch fresh mint for garnish

In an 8-quart bowl or nonreactive stockpot, combine the watermelon chunks, 3 cups of the strawberries, the lemon juice, sugar, and water.

Using an immersion blender on high speed, process until smooth and well blended, with no fruit chunks remaining. Alternatively, working in batches, ladle the mixture into a blender, cover securely, and process until smooth.

Slice the remaining 1$^1/_2$ cups strawberries and stir into the puréed watermelon mixture. Ladle the mixture into serving pitchers and refrigerate until well chilled, 3 to 4 hours.

Fill tall glasses with ice and then fill almost to the rim with the watermelon mixture. Make a cut halfway through the midpoint of each watermelon wedge, and balance a wedge over the rim of each glass. Garnish each glass with a mint sprig. Serve immediately.

SALADS

The salad is the closest connection between the garden and the table. Its ingredients are a gift of Mother Nature, and with a little help from cooks, one of our great avenues of culinary experimentation. In recent years, salads have evolved to a far greater degree than any other menu category, producing a treasure trove of wonderful new tastes and colors. The ability of a salad to deliver fresh textures and lovely flavors will help balance any meal that begs for something crisp, crunchy, and cold.

Our salad recipes range from the classic—an Italian bread salad—to the contemporary—asparagus and goat cheese. Some of them are ideal for beginning a meal or for serving as a side dish, while others are suitable as the main course, and still others can fill any of these menu roles. But in every case, they are guaranteed to please your guests.

Asparagus and Goat Cheese Salad

↦ serves 12 to 14 as a side dish

Light and simple salads are always appreciated on warm spring days. This salad combines the sweetness and depth of a vinaigrette flavored with cherry preserves and balsamic vinegar with the earthy tastes of asparagus and goat cheese. It is a versatile recipe, satisfying guests whether it is served as a main course, a first course, or as a side dish. MICHAEL THOMS

2 pounds asparagus

DARK CHERRY BALSAMIC VINAIGRETTE
$1/2$ cup balsamic vinegar
$1/4$ cup sugar
1 clove garlic, minced
$1/2$ cup cherry preserves
$1/4$ cup red wine vinegar
1 cup canola oil
Kosher salt
Freshly ground black pepper

1 head romaine lettuce, leaves separated, trimmed,
    and torn into bite-sized pieces
10 ounces mixed baby greens
$1/2$ cup pine nuts, toasted (see Cook's Note,
    page 123)
$1/2$ pound fresh goat cheese, crumbled
Kosher salt
Freshly ground black pepper

Select a pan large enough to accommodate the asparagus when lying flat. Fill the pan two-thirds full with water. Bring to a boil over high heat.

Snap off the woody bottom end of each asparagus spear, or trim all the spears to a uniform length. When the water is boiling, add the asparagus and cook, uncovered, until the spears are bright green and crisp-tender without tasting raw, 3 to 6 minutes, depending on the thickness of the spears. Test for doneness by inserting a paring knife into the thickest part of a spear or, easier still, by tasting one. Using tongs, immediately transfer the asparagus to a large bowl of ice water. Let cool for 1 to 2 minutes, and then drain and pat dry with paper towels. Cut the asparagus on the diagonal into $1^{1}/_{2}$ -inch lengths. Cover and refrigerate until needed.

To make the Dark Cherry Balsamic Vinaigrette, in a small saucepan over medium heat, combine the balsamic vinegar, sugar, and garlic and bring to a simmer, stirring frequently to dissolve the sugar. Simmer the mixture, uncovered, until reduced by half, about 10 minutes. Add the cherry preserves and cook for 1 minute longer. Remove from the heat and let cool to room temperature, then whisk in the red wine vinegar followed by the canola oil. Season to taste with salt and pepper. Set aside.

To assemble the salad, in a large bowl, combine the asparagus, romaine, mixed greens, most of the pine nuts, and most of the goat cheese. Drizzle 1 cup of the vinaigrette over the salad and toss gently to coat all the ingredients. Season to taste with salt and pepper. Using tongs, transfer the salad to chilled large salad bowls or plates (see Cook's Note, page 50), building height in the center and arranging the more colorful ingredients on top. Garnish with the remaining pine nuts and goat cheese. Serve immediately.

COOK'S NOTE: *The vinaigrette recipe yields about $2^{1}/_{2}$ cups dressing. Place extra dressing in a sealed jar and refrigerate for up to 2 weeks. Use on other salads, or drizzle over grilled shrimp or lobster.*

Lime and Cilantro Chicken Salad

↪ serves 6 as a main course or 12 as a first course

The secret of this salad lies in its dressing, which, when freshly made, provides a memorable flavor. We always use freshly squeezed lime juice for this dressing at Cafe Nordstrom, as none of the prepared products can compare to the explosion of flavor contributed by the fresh juice. FARIS ZOMA

CHIPOTLE-LIME VINAIGRETTE

1/3 cup seasoned rice wine vinegar

1/4 cup fresh lime juice

1 clove garlic, minced

2 teaspoons puréed chipotle chiles in adobo sauce
    (see Cook's Note)

2 tablespoons honey

1/2 teaspoon kosher salt

3/4 cup canola oil

1 cup chopped fresh cilantro stems and leaves

3 ears corn, shucked and grilled or boiled

1 1/4 pounds boneless, skinless chicken breasts,
    seasoned with salt and pepper, cooked,
    and julienned

1 1/2 cups diced plum tomatoes

1 pound mixed baby greens

2 cups (about 8 ounces) grated Jack cheese

1/2 cup chopped roasted red bell pepper
    (see Cook's Note, page 21)

Kosher salt

Freshly ground black pepper

3/4 cup toasted salted pumpkin seeds

Fresh cilantro sprigs for garnish

Lime wedges for serving

To make the Chipotle-Lime Vinaigrette, in a blender or in a food processor fitted with the metal blade, combine the vinegar, lime juice, garlic, chipotle chile, honey, and salt and process until thoroughly combined and smooth. With the machine running, gradually add the canola oil in a thin, steady stream to form an emulsion. Add the cilantro and pulse or process to combine. Taste and adjust the seasoning. Set aside.

To assemble the salad, cut off the corn kernels from the cobs: Working with 1 ear at a time, stand it upright, stem end down, on a cutting board. Using a sharp knife, cut downward along the cob, removing the kernels and rotating the cob a quarter turn after each cut. Discard the cobs and scoop the kernels into a large bowl. You should have about 2 cups.

Add the chicken, tomatoes, greens, Jack cheese, and bell pepper to the corn. Drizzle the vinaigrette over the salad and toss gently to coat all the ingredients. Season to taste with salt and pepper.

Using tongs, transfer the salad to chilled salad bowls (see Cook's Note), building height in the center. Scatter the pumpkin seeds evenly over the servings. Rest 1 or 2 cilantro sprigs on top of each salad and serve immediately. Pass the lime wedges at the table.

COOK'S NOTE: *Look for canned chipotle chiles (smoke-dried jalapeños) packed in adobo sauce (made from ground chile, herbs, tomato, and vinegar) in Latin markets or in the Mexican-food section in supermarkets.*

COOK'S NOTE: *A chilled salad bowl or plate keeps the salad cool and crisp, which makes a big difference in how it tastes. Simply pop a few plates into the freezer or refrigerator before beginning to make the salad.*